D0603808

WE ARE A THUNDERSTORM

WE ARE A THUNDERSTORM

written and photographed by

amity gaige

LANDMARK EDITIONS, INC.

P.O. Box 4469 • 1402 Kansas Avenue • Kansas City, Missouri 64127
(816) 241-4919

Dedicated to:
Madeline Tiger, who let me spell *above*, ''obove'';
Barbara Chimochowski, Jim Stahl,
and the others who encouraged me;
Morristown, New Jersey; Nepal;
and the Johns Hopkins University Center for the
Advancement of Academically Talented Youth.

Most of all,
to my sister, ''Precious'',
and to my mother and father
who helped make me what I am today.

811
GAI

15530

Third Printing

COPYRIGHT © 1990 BY AMITY GAIGE

International Standard Book Number: 0-933849-27-3 (LIB.BDG.)

Library of Congress Cataloging-in-Publication Data
Gaige, Amity, 1972-
  We are a thunderstorm / written and photographed by Amity Gaige.
  p.   cm.
  Poems and photographs present images of both fact and fancy.
ISBN 0-933849-27-3 (lib. bdg.)
  1. Children's poetry, American.   [1. American poetry.]
I. Title.
PS3557.A3518W4   1990   811'.54 — dc20   90-5922
                                                        CIP
                                                        AC

The publishers of WE ARE A THUNDERSTORM gratefully acknowledge the
courtesy of the following publishers for allowing us to reprint:
  ''The Flight'', CRICKET Magazine, April, 1986,
  (retitled ''The Encounter'', WE ARE A THUNDERSTORM, 1990);
  ''Hanging On'', SHOE TREE, Vol. 3, No. 1, Fall 1987;
  ''Trading'', MERLYN'S PEN, October/November, 1987;
  ''The Dancer'', CRICKET Magazine, January 8, 1988.

Editorial Coordinator: Nancy R. Thatch
Creative Coordinator: David Melton

Printed in the United States of America

Landmark Editions, Inc.
P.O. Box 4469
1402 Kansas Avenue
Kansas City, Missouri 64127
(816) 241-4919

WE ARE A THUNDERSTORM

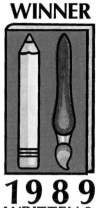

According to the Rules and Guidelines of The National Written & Illustrated by... Contest, books of poetry may be entered and photography is an acceptable form of illustration. Nevertheless, some participants wonder if poetry competes well with books of prose and if photographs are given the same consideration as drawings and paintings.

The publication of WE ARE A THUNDERSTORM, a book of poetry and photographs, should offer positive proof that the selection of winning books is not based on genre of text or media of illustration. The fact is, winners are chosen because of the superior quality of the works.

The quality of Amity Gaige's poetry and photographs is extraordinary. With an understanding beyond her years, she sensitively depicts both thought-provoking and humorous slices of life. Our judges were impressed with her broad range of skills and her ability to express social comments, introspective explorations, and sudden releases of quick humor. Her photographs are extensions of her poetic expression, blending split-second images of human emotions, lights and shadows, colors and tones.

Amity's beautiful book offers the reader profound experiences to be savored again and again.

— David Melton
Creative Coordinator
Landmark Editions, Inc.

BUTTERMINTS

It doesn't get much better —
buttermints on a wind-blown day,
when the iced October air
mingles them in your mouth
and makes you want to live forever.

Against the sapphire sky,
when bright leaves
fall like embers from the trees,
reach out and catch just one leaf
before it hits the ground.
Then make a wish.

There is so much to ask for —
a hundred prismed diamonds,
a team of sable stallions,
or a ladder to the moon.

Yet all you'll wish for
is another autumn day,
just like this one,
and one more
pocketful of buttermints.

THE DANCER

The sea is a dark dancer,
smooth and evermoving,
and I am bobbing
in my little boat
that sits upon her blue swells.

The sea is a dark dancer.
She lifts me on her heaving chest
and tickles my face
with salt-water spray.
She pushes me on
as a mother does a child,
to where the drifting clouds,
spread by a great butterknife,
meet the water.

The sea is a dark dancer,
with long graceful fingers
that comb her surface like dorsal fins.

And when she touches my reflection,
I wish that I could dive in
and dance with her.

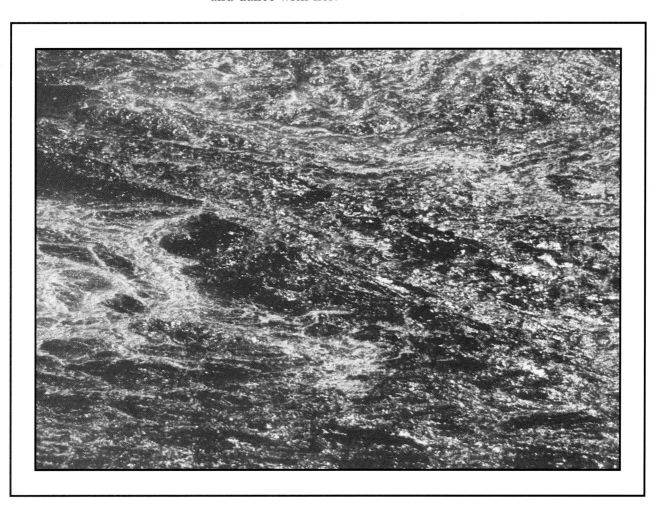

MEMORIES OF EDEN

In the spring
masses of wildflowers twined and bloomed,
calling our names with wide dragonfly mouths.
My sister and I would hear them
on those quiet, tree-toad nights,
and once the morning sun cast
Venetian blind patterns on our faces,
we'd put on sandals and run outside.
We'd race across the slippery grass
and enter the garden —
an Eden with red-ripe tomatoes
and pungent peppermint leaves
waiting to be clipped
for my mother's pilaf.
We'd sift through the pachysandra
in search of precious mica,
wreathe flowers in our hair,
and do cartwheels off a willow trunk
that had fallen during a storm.

The day we moved away,
I concluded
that the God who had loved me once
had changed his mind,
for my new place was neon-smudged and cold.
I missed the beckoning arms
of the knotty dogwood trees.
I missed the wheeze of fireplace wood
that warmed our feet as we lay on lambswool
and listened to happy Tchaikovsky.

I know my garden is gone;
my Eden has wilted with too many winters.
But I want to raise my children
in a place just like it,
so they, too, may have
an embracing garden to remember,
when their own green youths are done.

8

TIGER LILY

I know a girl named Tiger Lily
who does the Grape Dance in the sandbox
and sings the alphabet backwards.
She has hair, all at once red,
brown, and milky blonde,
and a happy face like a bouquet
of mismatched flowers.
She hasn't many friends —
except those in her head.
But they have a jolly time,
dressing up like gypsies and pirates,
and catching shadows in jars,
moonbeams in bottles,
and rainbows in teacups.

I don't remember being that young,
but if I ever was,
I hope
I was a Tiger Lily too.

CHANGING DESTINIES

On Saturdays
I visit the old Gypsy woman
who tells fortunes,
and when she turns her back,
I rearrange the tea leaves.

SIMPLE REQUESTS

Dear God,
will you please send more sunsets —
those big glowing light bulbs
that turn the sky nectarine colors?

And could I trouble you
for some clouds full of crystal rain
to wash away the summer dust?

And lastly,
could I have just one fat peach
without a worm?

TRADING

When Mina French-braided my hair,
she would entwine it
in her oriental fingers
and fondly pat its blond softness.
And I'd look up to admire
her silky black tresses.
Then, in our minds...
    we traded.

EDITH

Back in the backways,
curled in a fetal ball
like a sleeping house cat,
Edith dies in a doorway —
quietly, elusively,
like the waning of the moon.

Back in the backways,
where no one sees or cares,
Edith dies
again and again.
And she's dying right now
beneath the cold waning of the moon,
only under a different name
and in a different doorway.

MULTICOLORS

Be my daylight
and color my nighttimes gold.
Paint my cold ocean caves
a calm coral pink
and my shadowed corners
a vibrant red.
I need you now,
for my head is roaring
and tilting as if it holds
a small hurricane.
In the deepest of my private dark,
give me your multicolors.
So upon the cold swells
of my cruel and crashing ocean,
you can be my lighthouse,
and your beams shall melt
like yellow honey
upon my lonely head.

IN CHASE OF THE MONARCHS

Once, Ben and I
would chase the monarchs
in bleached copper
fields of wheat,
    then fall down together,
    breathless —
the way young boys do.

Then, those years were gone...
    but not Ben.
When I'd go to visit him,
he'd gently turn my face away
and mock the tears that rolled
    just for him.
My wheel-footed friend
would tell me not to worry.
    "We had our days
    for chasing monarchs," he'd say.

Now, I smile at faded photographs
    of Ben and me —
ones that only he and I would understand.
Ben's laughter runs through my mind
    like a memorized poem.
    And my old shoulders
    slump with sorrow
because the chase of the monarchs
seems a hundred years gone....
    but, then...
    so does Ben.

TOMMY MAHONEY

tommy mahoney was a tiny tot
with orange hair and an untied shoe.
He used to *pickhisnose* and *wethisbed* —
two terrible diseases
about which everyone made fun of him.
The other boys,
who were big enough for stick ball
and staying out past dark,
would smirk, "Here comes tommy mahoney —
the *pickhisnose* and *wethisbed*."
Then they'd laugh, "Ha! Ha!"
They thought tommy mahoney would
nevergrow,
which is also an awful disease.

Till suddenly,
in the space of a summer's vacation,
he grew a whole yard taller.
Then he was TOMMY MAHONEY
and quite large at that.
The other boys would say,
"Hullo, TOMMY MAHONEY.
How about a game of stick ball?"
But TOMMY was too preoccupied
with being careful
not to catch their hair
in his shoelaces,
for it was such a nuisance
when they groveled at his feet that way.

LINEN MOTHER

Carry me,
carry me,
linen-closet-clean Mother,
pious and pale,
poor and pressed with starch,
penny-pinching,
potato-faced.
Smile at me, honeysuckle woman,
for in your fuzzy cotton frocks,
you wear your own kind of satin.

SIDEWALK SONG

Silhouettes —
Slim against the skidding sun.

Sidewalks —
Cold like a scream.

Figures —
Lurking in shadowed doorways.

Hats —
Hugging heads like dark halos.

Breath —
Steaming from angry mouths.

Rumble —
Switch blades flashing, no place to run.

Pain —
There's no such thing as a black rose.

Mama —
I won't be home tonight.

SAD POEMS

It's evening — the time
when the world hesitates.
Clouds stall and hush,
and the Earth strikes
a chord of euphony
in the blush of the sun.

And I don't want to write
sad poems anymore.

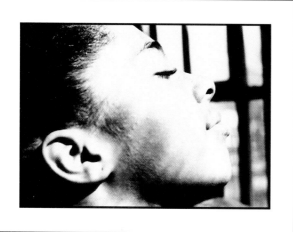

I WANT

I want
something that feels like childhood —
something that coos in the sunlight
and gurgles like a rain gutter at night;
something that hangs among my ferns
and smells like clover,
and cinnamon apples,
and lemon custard pie.

And I want something that's
emerald, purple, and gentle blue,
that's sprinkled with gold
and sugar coated,
with a tail like a comet
when it races across the sky,
and warm embracing arms
to comfort me when I cry.

I want it to push me on the tire swing
and sit on my feet when they're cold.
It will talk to me
when my world is not beautiful,
then sing me to sleep
with a voice made of silver wind chimes.

HANGING ON

I'm just a little Southern boy,
stuck like a refrigerator magnet
to my papa's pant leg.
When gentle breezes blow,
I nestle my face
against its denim softness.
But if the wind tries to whip me over,
I hold fast like a sand crab,
and Papa's leg becomes a pillar
of pebbles glued together.
And when black funnels in the sky
come rumbling down the fields,
uprooting lifetimes
and blowing them away,
I shake like jelly
and pray for the life of me
that Papa's leg can run fast.

16

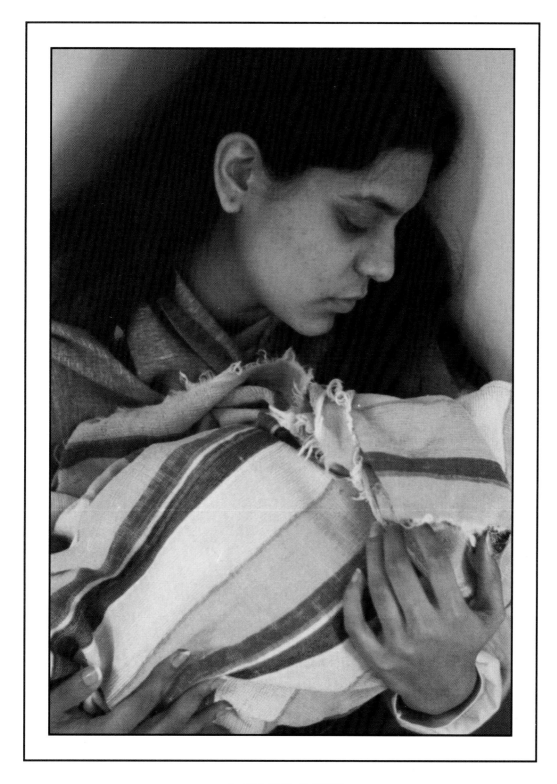

A HARD LIFE

The sad brown woman
with the hungry baby
cradles his thin head.
And when she looks up at me,
her face
is a book
of mournful poetry.

WHEN I DIE

When I die,
bury me in
something comfortable
and put flowers
in my hands.

When I die,
bury me quietly
where cathedral trees
shower their golden harvest
upon the tender ground.

Then take a single flower
from my grave,
and whisper
just above the wind
that you love me.

When I die.

OCEAN SKY

The sky is
a delicate blue,
that if eaten
would melt in your mouth
like a sugar wafer.
Clouds slide across it.
They are ships,
and the world is underwater.

I LOVE YOU WHEN

I love you when
the deer sing in the quiet.
I love you when
the trees grow vines around the moon.
I love you when
you make the rain taste like grape ice.

I love you.

I love you when
the ivy yawns against the golden wind.
I love you when
the rain makes purple fish in the ocean.
I love you
when you catch the stars for me to hold.

I love you.

20

THE ENCOUNTER

So close did my father come to Death one day,
that if Death had been a still pool
and my father had been a bird,
his wings would've skimmed the smooth surface
close enough to ripple the water.
I remember Death
looming in the air like a burnt smell,
like a bad cat, waiting.
But my father recovered,
and now I see,
not only was I afraid of Death,
but Death must have been afraid of me.

THE AMARYLLIS IS WILTING

The amaryllis is wilting.
Its red petals are
stretched out like drying linen,
nodding slowly.
The tall stiff stalk is tilting,
and the drooping buds
don't smell anymore.

So, I called to tell you,
    "The amaryllis is wilting."
Actually, I called because I miss you.

But for now,
    the amaryllis is wilting.
It has faded into paler shades.
Soon it will stand bare
in the dark of winter.
I feel rather bare myself —
    now that the room is cold and empty,
    now that you are gone,
    and now that the
    amaryllis is wilting.

ROSES AGAINST THE GRAY

There are children wading on a distant shore,
sending roses on the gentle tide.
They set them down on soft sand
for the waves to gather and sweep into the ocean.
The crimson roses bob on the surface
with the bored gray gulls
and finally float across the waters
to lose their innocence
upon a pale polluted beach.

DO IT NOW!

It's your turn
to take a bite of purple plums
and those forbidden fruits
intended for the table centerpiece.

Life is a bush of plump and pleasing berries.
Make jam!

HEY, MARGIE

Hey, Margie,
Hey, Babe,
ain't it a nice day!
Gimme a slice
of that great apple pie!

    Hey,
    sorry that black fella had to die.
    I know,
    it was messy in fronta your store, but...

Oh,
could you gimme a little bit more
of that de-e-e-licious coffee.

    You know how it is —
    we cain't have 'em
    mixin' in with our kids.

Yeah,
decaf for sure,
just a little bit more.

    Next time we'll get one
    by some other store.

Yeah,
milk will be fine,
and a little bit sweet.

    Say,
    I sure looked neat
    in my big white sheet.

Thanks, thanks a lot.
That sure hit the spot.

    Bye, Margie,
    Bye, Darlin' —
    see y'all in the mornin'.

SYLVIA

The teacher showed the kids
a sheet of paper
that had a red dot
in the middle of a yellow space.

Then,
he asked them
to describe what they saw.

All the kids said,
 "Looks like someone
  put a red dot on
  a yellow piece of paper!"

But not Sylvia.
She said,
 "I see a rose in a cornfield."

THE CLOSET MONSTER

As a child,
I recall
leaving the closet door open,
for I knew
if I closed the door,
I would become afraid of
what was behind it.

Now I've outgrown
such childish fears
and foolish superstitions.
So where has
my homeless closet monster gone?
It probably lurks
in some other child's
darkened closet,
    or...
      under my bed.

A NOTE FROM JILL

Behold us!
A mighty pair are we,
skipping hand in hand
down the hillside steep.
No Tweedle-dum
and Tweedle-dee
are we.
But Romulus and Remus,
Sita and Ram,
sure and proud,
strong and swift.

But remember, Jack,
how you broke your crown
the last time you tripped.

A WINTER DREAM

In my winter dream,
a ghostly echo ebbs and flows
between the branches
of shivering trees.
It forms blue icicles
in my mind
and sighs like a hollow wind
in my heart.

I would rather
   dream of spring.

OLD PEOPLE

Old people smell of
fabric softener and tonic.
Sun-tanned, smiling, spectacled,
powdered, permed or combed —
mine are always kind and
wear white undershirts,
or if they're women, pearls.
They look beyond what I can see
and understand what I cannot.
They pop my bubbles,
do magic tricks with quarters,
eat oatmeal cookies,
and never swat at flies.
They
   drive too slow...
   talk too soft...
   cry too much...
      go too soon.

PLEASE

Please,
don't lead me blindly
to a strange and empty place.
Please,
don't run
when I plead for you to walk.
Please,
curl your big hand around my little one
and guide me to the starting line.
I'll go on from there.

When the starting shot cries,
I pray you will not hold me back
and sob sad good-byes.
By the time you let go,
I will have lost the race.

UNWRITTEN

Out there,
somewhere,
there is a poem
that runs like
a river down the mountain.
It has no name; it has no home.
While it would love to sing,
it has no voice.
While it would love to dance,
it has no form.
So it wanders aimlessly,
out there,
somewhere,
in the far beyond.
And despite its promise,
it still remains
unwritten.

THE WRITER

He props his head up
for a brief moment
and smells the ink
boiling upon the page.
His eyes narrow to consider
the glimmer of a thought.
Then, with his pen in hand,
he molds that thought
into words,
which proves —
there is still magic in the world.

WE ARE A THUNDERSTORM

Individually,
  we are single drops of rain,
  falling silently into the dust,
  offering scant promise
  of moisture to the thirsty land.

But, together,
  we can nourish the Earth
  and revive its hopes and dreams.

Together,
  we are a thunderstorm.

BOOKS FOR STUDENTS
– WINNERS OF THE NATIONAL WRITTEN &

by Aruna Chandrasekhar, age 9
Houston, Texas

A touching and timely story! When the lives of many otters are threatened by a huge oil spill, a group of concerned people come to their rescue. Wonderful illustrations.
Printed Full Color
ISBN 0-933849-33-8

by Anika D. Thomas, age 13
Pittsburgh, Pennsylvania

A compelling autobiography! A young girl's heartrending account of growing up in a tough, inner-city neighborhood. The illustrations match the mood of this gripping story.
Printed Two Colors
ISBN 0-933849-34-6

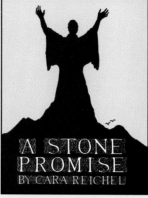

by Cara Reichel, age 15
Rome, Georgia

Elegant and eloquent! A young stonecutter vows to create a great statue for his impoverished village. But his fame almost stops him from fulfilling that promise.
Printed Two Colors
ISBN 0-933849-35-4

by Jonathan Kahn, age 9
Richmond Heights, Ohio

A fascinating nature story! While Patulous, a prairie rattlesnake, searches for food, he must try to avoid the claws and fangs of his own enemies.
Printed Full Color
ISBN 0-933849-36-2

by Adam Moore, age 9
Broken Arrow, Oklahoma

A remarkable true story! When Adam was eight years old, he fell and ran an arrow into his head. With rare insight and humor, he tells of his ordeal and his amazing recovery.
Printed Two Colors
ISBN 0-933849-24-9

by Michael Aushenker, age 19
Ithaca, New York

Chomp! Chomp! When Arthur forgets to feed his goat, the animal eats everything in sight. A very funny story — good to the last bite. The illustrations are terrific.
Printed Full Color
ISBN 0-933849-28-1

by Leslie Ann MacKeen, age 9
Winston-Salem, North Carolina

Loaded with fun and puns! When Jeremiah T. Fitz's car stops running, several animals offer suggestions for fixing it. The results are hilarious. The illustrations are charming.
Printed Full Color
ISBN 0-933849-19-2

by Elizabeth Haidle, age 13
Beaverton, Oregon

A very touching story! The grumpiest Elfkin learns to cherish the friendship of others after he helps an injured snail and befriends an orphaned boy. Absolutely beautiful.
Printed Full Color
ISBN 0-933849-20-6

by Amy Hagstrom, age 9
Portola, California

An exciting western! When a boy and an old Indian try to save a herd of wild ponies, they discover a lost canyon and see the mystical vision of the Great White Stallion.
Printed Full Color
ISBN 0-933849-15-X

by Isaac Whitlatch, age 11
Casper, Wyoming

The true confessions of a devout vegetable hater! Isaac tells ways to avoid and dispose of the "slimy green things." His colorful illustrations provide a salad of laughter and mirth.
Printed Full Color
ISBN 0-933849-16-8

by Dav Pilkey, age 19
Cleveland, Ohio

A thought-provoking parable! Two kings halt an arms race and learn to live in peace. This outstanding book launched Dav's career. He now has seven more books published.
Printed Full Color
ISBN 0-933849-22-2

by Karen Kerber, age 12
St. Louis, Missouri

A delightfully playful book! The text is loaded with clever alliterations and gentle humor. Karen's brightly colored illustrations are composed of wiggly and waggly strokes of genius.
Printed Full Color
ISBN 0-933849-29-X

Your Students Will Love These Wonderful Books!

BY STUDENTS!®

ILLUSTRATED BY... AWARDS FOR STUDENTS –

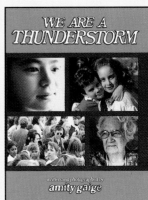

by Jayna Miller, age 19
Zanesville, Ohio

The funniest Halloween ever! When Hammer the Rabbit takes all the treats, his friends get even. Their hilarious scheme includes a haunted house and mounds of chocolate.
Printed Full Color
ISBN 0-933849-37-0

by Lauren Peters, age 7
Kansas City, Missouri

The Christmas that almost wasn't! When Santa Claus takes a vacation, Mrs. Claus and the elves go on strike. Toys aren't made. Cookies aren't baked. Super illustrations.
Printed Full Color
ISBN 0-933849-25-7

by Michael Cain, age 11
Annapolis, Maryland

A glorious tale of adventure! To become a knight, a young man must face a beast in the forest, a spell-binding witch, and a giant bird that guards a magic oval crystal.
Printed Full Color
ISBN 0-933849-26-5

by Amity Gaige, age 16
Reading, Pennsylvania

A lyrical blend of poetry and photographs! Amity's sensitive poems offer thought-provoking ideas and amusing insights. This lovely book is one to be savored and enjoyed.
Printed Full Color
ISBN 0-933849-27-3

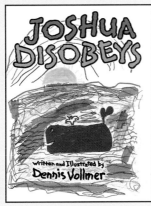

by Heidi Salter, age 19
Berkeley, California

Spooky and wonderful! To save her vivid imagination, a young girl must confront the Great Grey Grimly himself. The narrative is filled with suspense. Vibrant illustrations.
Printed Full Color
ISBN 0-933849-21-4

by Dennis Vollmer, age 6
Grove, Oklahoma

A baby whale's curiosity gets him into a lot of trouble. GUINNESS BOOK OF RECORDS lists Dennis as the youngest author/illustrator of a published book.
Printed Full Color
ISBN 0-933849-12-5

by Lisa Gross, age 12
Santa Fe, New Mexico

A touching story of self-esteem! A puppy is laughed at because of his unusual appearance. His search for acceptance is told with sensitivity and humor. Wonderful illustrations.
Printed Full Color
ISBN 0-933849-13-3

by Stacy Chbosky, age 14
Pittsburgh, Pennsylvania

A powerful plea for freedom! This emotion-packed story of a young slave touches an essential part of the human spirit. Made into a film by Disney Educational Productions.
Printed Full Color
ISBN 0-933849-14-1

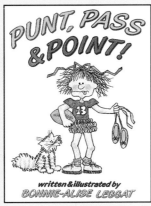

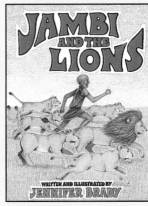

by David McAdoo, age 14
Springfield, Missouri

An exciting intergalactic adventure! In the distant future, a courageous warrior defends a kingdom from a dragon from outer space. Astounding sepia illustrations.
Printed Duotone
ISBN 0-933849-23-0

by Bonnie-Alise Leggat, age 8
Culpeper, Virginia

Amy J. Kendrick wants to play football, but her mother wants her to become a ballerina. Their clash of wills creates hilarious situations. Clever, delightful illustrations.
Printed Full Color
ISBN 0-933849-39-7

by Lisa Kirsten Butenhoff, age 13
Woodbury, Minnesota

The people of a Russian village face the winter without warm clothes or enough food. Then their lives are improved by a young girl's gifts. A tender story with lovely illustrations.
Printed Full Color
ISBN 0-933849-40-0

by Jennifer Brady, age 17
Columbia, Missouri

When poachers capture a pride of lions, a native boy tries to free the animals. A skillfully told story. Glowing illustrations illuminate this African adventure.
Printed Full Color
ISBN 0-933849-41-9

They Will Want to Read and Enjoy All of Them! ORDER NOW!

Jayna Miller
age 19

Lauren Peters
age 7

Michael Cain
age 11

Heidi Salter
age 19

Amity Gaige
age 16

Dennis Vollmer
age 6

Lisa Gross
age 12

Stacy Chbosky
age 14

Karen Kerber
age 12

David McAdoo
age 14

THE WINNERS OF THE 1992 NATIONAL
WRITTEN & ILLUSTRATED BY... AWARDS FOR STUDENTS

FIRST PLACE	**FIRST PLACE**	**FIRST PLACE**	**GOLD AWARD**	**GOLD AWARD**
6–9 Age Category	10–13 Age Category	14–19 Age Category	Publisher's Selection	Publisher's Selection
Benjamin Kendall	**Steven Shepard**	**Travis Williams**	**Dubravka Kolanović'**	**Amy Jones**
age 7	age 13	age 16	age 18	age 17
State College, Pennsylvania	Great Falls, Virginia	Sardis, B.C., Canada	Savannah, Georgia	Shirley, Arkansas

   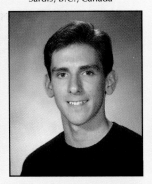 

ALIEN INVASIONS

When Ben puts on a new super-hero costume, he starts seeing Aliens who are from outer space. His attempts to stop the pesky invaders provide loads of laughs. The colorful illustrations add to the fun!

29 Pages, Full Color
ISBN 0 933849 42 7

FOGBOUND

A gripping thriller! When a boy rows his boat to an island to retrieve a stolen knife, he must face threatening fog, treacherous currents, and a sinister lobsterman. Outstanding illustrations!

29 Pages, Two-Color
ISBN 0 933849 43 5

CHANGES

A chilling mystery! When a teen-age boy discovers his classmates are missing, he becomes entrapped in a web of conflicting stories, false alibis, and frightening changes. Dramatic ink drawings!

29 Pages, Two-Color
ISBN 0 933849 44 3

A SPECIAL DAY

Ivan enjoys a wonderful day in the country with his grandparents, a dog, a cat, and a delightful bear that is *always* hungry. Cleverly written, brilliantly illustrated! Little kids will love this book!

29 Pages, Full Color
ISBN 0 933849 45 1

ABRACADABRA

A whirlwind adventure! An enchanted unicorn helps a young girl rescue her eccentric aunt from the evil Sultan of Zabar. A charming story, with lovely illustrations that add a magical glow!

29 Pages, Full Color
ISBN 0 933849 46 X

BOOKS FOR STUDENTS BY STUDENTS! ®

LANDMARK EDITIONS, INC.
P.O. BOX 4469 • KANSAS CITY, MISSOURI 64127 • (816) 241-4919